150 YEARS OF WORCESTER:

 1848-1998

150 YEARS OF WORCESTER:

 1848-1998

Albert B. Southwick

Chandler House Press
Worcester, Massachusetts
USA

150 Years of Worcester: 1848-1998

ISBN 1-886284-16-4
Library of Congress Catalog Card Number 97-78120
First Edition
ABCDEFGHIJK

Published by
Chandler House Press
335 Chandler Street
Worcester, MA 01602
USA

President
Lawrence J. Abramoff

Publisher/Editor-in-Chief
Richard J. Staron

Vice President of Sales, Publishing and Distribution
Irene S. Bergman

Editorial/Production Manager
Jennifer J. Goguen

Book Design
Andrea Stowe

Cover Design
Janet Amorello

Cover
Looking East from Denny Hill, a painting by Ralph Earl
Worcester Art Museum
Worcester, Massachusetts
Museum purchase

Author Photo
Peter Hagberg

Chandler House Press books are available at special discounts for bulk purchases. For more information about how to arrange such purchases, please contact Irene Bergman at Chandler House Press, 335 Chandler Street, Worcester, MA 01602, or call (800) 642-6657, or fax (508) 756-9425, or find us on the World Wide Web at www.tatnuck.com.

To Shirley

ACKNOWLEDGMENTS

This book was written with the substantial help and encouragement of various individuals and organizations. My gratitude particularly goes to Bruce Bennett, Allen Fletcher, William Wallace, Kenneth Moynihan, Nancy Gaudette, Vincent Powers, Michael Moore, Jack Larkin, George LaBonte, Larry Abramoff, William Short, Stephen O'Neil, Sande Bishop, Donald Chamberlayne and the helpful staff people of the Worcester Historical Museum, the American Antiquarian Society, the Worcester Room of the Worcester Public Library and the Telegram & Gazette. The members of the Worcester History Group at Assumption have been a constant source of information and encouragement. I thank them all.

Worcester, Massachusetts sign, Webster Square
(© Brian F. Crowley)

WORCESTER IN 1848

Eighteen-forty-eight was quite a year. It brought violent revolutions to France, Austria, Italy, Germany and other parts of Europe, which sent new waves of immigrants to America. It saw the United States annex an enormous chunk of Mexico, including what is now California, New Mexico, Colorado and Arizona, setting off a renewed national firestorm over slavery. Karl Marx published his *Communist Manifesto* in 1848, at about the same time that gold was discovered in California.

And in 1848, the town of Worcester became a city, with a mayor, board of aldermen and a city council. It had one street that was partly paved (Main Street from the Common to Lincoln Square), about 17,000 residents and one bathtub. Things were about to change.

Worcester, which contained perhaps 200 settlers in 1718, had grown steadily but slowly over the generations—to 2,400 in 1800, about 3,000 in 1820, 4,000 in 1830 and almost 7,500 in 1840. But then began the population explosion that would last for a century. The bustling village of 1840 doubled its head count in the next eight years, putting growing pressures on the society and its infrastructure. The opening of the Blackstone Canal in 1828 had given it a shot in the arm. Then the railroads came, changing Worcester forever. The Boston & Worcester Railroad rolled into town in 1835 to much hoopla. By 1848 Worcester was served by trains to Norwich, Albany and Providence, with connections to Nashua and Fitchburg near completion. Within months, 24 trains a day would be pulling in and out of Worcester, making it the crossroads of New England. The daily *Worcester Spy* took to calling Worcester "Rail Road City."

By 1847 the town was growing so fast that the town fathers decided that the old board of selectmen had to be replaced by something better. Despite the opposition of some farmers, who feared that a city form of government meant higher taxes, most of the residents wanted a better system. At town meeting on Nov. 8, 1847, "on motion of John Milton Earle, it was voted that a committee of ten be appointed to draw up and present to the Legislature a petition for a city charter." Earle, a Whig bigwig, was owner and editor of the *Worcester Daily Spy* and constant booster of Worcester.

Things happened fast after that. The legislation was signed by the governor on Feb. 29, 1848 and approved by Worcester voters on March 18 by a vote of 1,026 to 487. The first city election was held on April 9, and Mayor Levi Lincoln and the new board of aldermen were sworn in on April 17. Seldom has Worcester accomplished so much in six weeks.

The new government had its work cut out. According to the report of the Committee on Finance, "The Treasury was empty and a debt outstanding against the city of $99,677. By the charter, the city was to assume all the liabilities of the Town of Worcester, the Centre School District, and the Aqueduct Corporation." Also, the new cycle of explosive growth would quintuple Worcester's population in the next 50 years and eventually make it the second largest city in New England. The 7,500 Worcesterites in 1840 had increased to almost 17,000 by 1848, and the inflow kept swelling by the month, thanks largely to the flood of immigrants from famine-stricken Ireland.

We would find the Worcester of 1848 vastly different but recognizable. Access to the village from the east was by the road around the north end of Lake Quinsigamond (now Lincoln Street), straight across the lake on the old floating bridge (Route 9), or by the Boston & Worcester Railroad skirting the south end of the lake. The principal roads were Main Street, Summer Street, Central Street, Thomas Street,

School Street, Mechanic Street, Green Street, Water Street, Grafton Street, Pine (now Shrewsbury) Street, West Boylston Street, Millbrook Street, and Pleasant Street. The Common was bounded by Front Street on the north side, Main Street on the west side, South (now Franklin) Street on the south side and Church Street on the east. The recently abandoned Blackstone Canal, fetid, polluted and home of large wharf rats, still ran down the village center, from its basin terminus at Central and Thomas Streets, to the Blackstone River at Water Street. Except for the central village, Worcester was mostly a farming community with fields and woods and pastures connected by dirt roads and cowpaths.

Worcester, which was to become a conglomerate of more than 30 nationalities, then had only two main ethnic groups—those stemming from England and Scotland and those from Ireland, with only a smattering of French from Canada. The Protestant Yankees had been here from the settling of the town in the early 1700s. The Irish, steadfastly Roman Catholic, had arrived in the 1820s to work on the Blackstone Canal and then the railroads. (They may not have been the first from the Emerald Isle. One old account says that "John Young, an Irishman, aged 107 years" was buried in the old Thomas Street graveyard in 1730. If so, he was perhaps the first Irishman to make Worcester his home). By 1848, the Irish numbered perhaps 2,000. Had it not been for events abroad, they might have remained a small minority of Worcester's population. But in 1845-46, a blight wiped out the Irish potato crop. In the years following, at least one million Irish people starved to death and perhaps two million more fled their stricken land. At least a million found their way to the United States in the next few years. When some of them, sick, destitute and dying, arrived in Worcester, they were put up temporarily in St. John's Church, just newly dedicated.

How many Irish were in Worcester in 1848? There are no solid statistics. But Dr. Vincent Powers, the scholar of the Irish experience in Worcester, has estimated that Worcester Irish numbered about 500

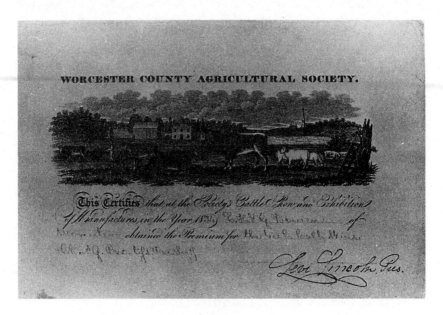

The Worcester County Agricultural Society was one of the most important community organizations in 1848.

The first railroad station in Worcester was at the corner of Foster and Norwich streets.

The United States Arms Hotel was built in 1784 and
hosted President George Washington when he visited
Worcester in 1789. It was later renamed the Exchange
Hotel and gave its name to Exchange Street.

The Oread Institute, completed in 1849, was one of the
first colleges for women in the country.

in 1845 and between 1,000 and 2,000 in 1848. Between 1847 and 1850, the stream of Irish immigrants became a flood, and by the end of 1850 there probably were at least 3,000 Irish people in Worcester. They were on their way to becoming the largest and most influential ethnic group in Worcester, a distinction they retained 150 years later.

The ghastliness of the Irish famine was borne in on Worcester residents by a series of dispatches published in the *Spy*, and written by Elihu Burritt, Worcester's famed "learned blacksmith" who was on a lecture tour in Europe. He called Ireland "this region of the shadow of death" and gave accounts as grim as those from Ethiopia in the 1980s.

On February 16, 1847, an Irish "Relief Meeting" was held at Worcester's Town Hall, "the largest such meeting ever held in this town" according to the *Spy*. Levi Lincoln was in the chair, and the committee appointed was the cream of the Worcester establishment—Isaac Davis, Edward Earle, Thomas Kinnicutt, Ichabod Washburn, James Estabrook, Albert Curtis, Francis H. Dewey, Alonzo Hill, Edward Everett Hale, Ira Barton and others, along with St. John's pastor, Rev. Matthew Gibson, and Holy Cross President James Ryder. The committee was charged with taking up a collection in Worcester, and also "to correspond with all the towns in the county for the purpose of inviting their cooperation with us in this benevolent undertaking…."

The *Spy* reported that, even before the meeting, "The Catholic Society in this town has already raised and forwarded $300 and they intend making it up to $1,000."

Although the Irish Catholics in Worcester would suffer prejudice and discrimination for years to come, that 1847 meeting showed that many prominent Worcester Yankees early on were willing to accept the Irish as fellow citizens worthy of respect. It was a tradition that endured. When Holy Cross petitioned the Legislature for a charter in 1865, Isaac Davis, Alexander Bullock and Elijah B. Stoddard signed the petition and made sure it moved smoothly through the Legislature. Years after that, U.S. Senator George Frisbie Hoar became an eloquent champion of the Irish, whom he deeply admired. That is part of the complex story of the Irish in Worcester.

For the first 63 years after it was established as a town in 1722, Worcester had only one church—the meeting house on the Common, later known as Old South Church. In 1785 the Second Parish Church (now First Unitarian) split off amid a noisy controversy. By 1848, the city also had, according to Henry J. Howland, an early Worcester publisher, a Catholic Church (St. John's), a Baptist church, a Calvinist Society, two Episcopal churches, a Methodist church, a Universalist Society, a Quaker meeting, a Union church, and "one or two Societies of colored persons."

In 1842, after two days here, Charles Dickens had described Worcester as a pleasant little village "with an aspect of newness on every object… All the buildings looked as if they had been built and painted that morning…."

Six years later, the pleasant little village was being swamped by the hordes of new people and businesses, and things didn't look so pristine. Behind the Town Hall and the First Church on Main Street, the Common was an unsightly mix of gravestones, school buildings, rubbish piles, peddler stalls and the tracks of the Norwich & Worcester Railroad. The dirt roads, including Main Street, were rutted and rocky, plagued with clouds of dust in dry weather, deep mud when it rained and dotted with horse manure at all times. (Not only horse manure, either. One of the first ordinances passed by the new city government recodified an old bylaw that banned pigs, sheep and cows from city streets.) When the selectmen in 1847 decided to pave Main Street from the Common to Lincoln Square, the committee in charge recommended "round stone paving" instead of "square stone paving" on grounds of economy. The new system of "McAdamizing" was rejected as too expensive and unproven. The round stone paving was probably tooth-rattling for those who traveled over it in their iron-wheeled wagons and buggies. But that was better than getting stuck in the mud.

The Chase Building was the largest and grandest office building in Worcester when it was built in 1886.

Insane Hospital, Worcester, Mass.

The Insane Hospital, later Worcester State Hospital, became one of the largest hospitals in the state when the Belmont Street addition opened in the 1870s.

LINCOLN SQUARE, WORCESTER, MASS., WITH A VIEW OF THE NEW ANTIQUARIAN HALL, OLD AND NEW COURT HOUSES, AND UNITARIAN CHURCH.

Lincoln Square around 1850

The Salisbury Mansion in Lincoln Square. The Salisbury House, built in 1835 by Stephen Salisbury, is at the far left. The Central Congregational Church (later United Congregational) is at right rear. (from the collections of the Worcester Historical Museum)

Water was another issue. Although most Worcester homes and businesses were still relying on private or public wells, a Worcester Aqueduct Company had been formed in 1845 to pipe water from Bladder Pond to the downtown neighborhood. (Bladder Pond, an unfortunate designation for a water supply, was soon renamed Bell Pond). By 1848, when the newly-established city took it over, the Aqueduct Company had laid 14,000 feet of pipe and installed 58 hydrants. The new water system had enabled the fire department to battle two major fires on Main Street in 1847. According to tradition, Worcester already had at least one bathtub, located in the Trumbull house, once the historic second court house and now a private home on Massachusetts Avenue. Folklore has it that George Trumbull decided to expand his house in the 1840s and included in his plans a "bathing room."

Curiously, therapeutic baths and bathing became quite a fad in the 1840s. The *National Aegis* instructed its readers to bathe, and bathe frequently: "If you would avoid colds... bathe. If you would enjoy your youth, blitheness of limb and cheer of spirits, bathe frequently... If you would preserve your digestion and enjoy the good things of life, bathe."

Personal hygiene in those days would not have impressed us. A bath once a week in a clothes washtub was probably the best that most families could accomplish.

One of the main problems facing the new city government was what to do with the water (Mill Brook, the Blackstone Canal) flowing through the center of downtown, from Salisbury (Institute) Pond to the Blackstone River. Two years previously, the Blackstone Canal Company had sold the Massachusetts portion of the waterway to the Providence & Worcester Railroad for $22,500. But the railroad had no obligation to maintain the various bridges and channels. A study committee investigated and reported that much work needed to be done to keep the stream from flooding periodically, particularly at

Lincoln Square and Green Street. The long filling in of the old canal soon began, and a century later, the stream was underground and out of mind except during times of hurricanes and floods, such as 1955.

Charles Dickens in 1842 had traveled down a Main Street lined with private homes as well as business establishments. Between the Salisbury mansion in Lincoln Square and John Milton Earle's house at the corner of Main and Chatham Streets were the residences of some of Worcester's leading citizens. By 1848, Main Street was going commercial and some of those leading citizens were moving a few blocks west, up Elm Street, Pleasant Street, Chatham Street and Highland Street. The Salisburys had led the westward movement when they abandoned their old mansion in Lincoln Square and moved a block up the hill to their elegant new domicile (in 1998 the headquarters of the Red Cross). Despite Dickens' patronizing comments, Worcester had many substantial buildings. In addition to several hotels, Main Street had the Butman Block, Brinley Hall, the Central Exchange Building and other office buildings devoted to commerce and the professions. Manufacturing plants were located mainly in the Union Street and Lincoln Square complex of brick buildings owned by Stephen Salisbury and William Merrifield, where a central steam engine drove a system of pulleys and belts that manufacturers could rent by the horsepower. A harbinger of things to come was Ichabod Washburn's wire mill on Grove Street, where so much of Worcester's industrial future was being founded on Washburn's inventions and improvements to the process of drawing wire.

The 1840s saw the rise of a new class in Worcester. These were the "mechanics," meaning the architects, inventors, draftsmen, machinists, toolmakers and entrepreneurs who would make Worcester a prime engine of the Industrial Revolution. The Worcester County Mechanics Association, founded in 1842, immediately began hosting a series of lectures and collecting a technical library for its members. On July 26, 1848, the association announced that its "First Exhibition for the encouragement of Manufactures and the Mechanic Arts, will be holden at City Hall... on Tuesday... being the week of the annual Cattle Show...." The Cattle Show on the Common had long been one of the town's significant annual events. But in the years to come, agriculture would be gradually displaced by the "Mechanic Arts," especially after the construction of Mechanics Hall by the Mechanics Association nine years later.

By 1848, Worcester's coming industrial power was already in evidence. The 1840s were marked by inventors and entrepreneurs crowding into Worcester, ready for fame and fortune. They had names like Heald, Crompton, Curtis, Marble, Cœs, Boutwell, Ware, Pratt, Knowlton, Hawes, Sargent and Elwood Adams. William Wheeler had already installed a steam engine at his foundry. Henry J. Howland, a Worcester publisher, printed a short guidebook to Worcester in 1850. Among the city's manufactures he listed: "Woolen, Paper and other machinery, Machinists' Tools, Iron and Brass Wire, various Woolen Goods, Boots and Shœs... Plows and other Agricultural Implements... Musical Instruments, Castings of all kinds, Fire Arms, Copying Presses, Screw Wrenches, Hammers, Augurs, Knives and Chisels, Binders' Shears, Picture Frames, Porte Monnaies, Fancy Boxes, Fancy Cards, and almost innumerable other articles...." The firm with the largest number of employees was Luther Freeland & Co., a merchant tailor located near Lincoln Square. The company employed 300 people, 250 of them women, manufacturing ready-made clothes. Worcester had half a dozen makers of ready-made clothing, employing perhaps 500 workers overall. Average pay for full-time help was about ten dollars a month.

Prof. Vincent Powers has calculated that day laborers in 1848 made between 30 and 75 cents a day, depending on the line of work. Skilled workers got more, maybe as much as one dollar a day.

The new city also boasted five banks, four insurance companies, and a wide array of goods and services from lawyers, doctors, bootmakers, wheelwrights, farriers, blacksmiths, dental plate makers, liverymen, harness makers, farmers and dozens of other suppliers. Worcester citizens had a choice of three daguerreotype establishments if they wanted their pictures taken. They could take French lessons from M. Jaques Troyon, located at 20 Central Street. And, wonder of wonders, "painless dentistry" had arrived. Two Worcester dentists were advertising tooth extraction with chloroform, the "recently discovered substitute for ether." Dental work, particularly extractions, had been a painful nightmare for centuries.

Judging from other historical accounts of American life at that time, it seems likely that Worcester teeth were nothing to brag about. Plenty of Worcester folk probably displayed rotten or missing teeth and foul gums. An old person with all of his teeth in place was probably considered remarkable. And lots of Worcester folk displayed blotched and scrofulous skin, along with pockmarks from smallpox or chicken pox. Impetigo and head lice were probably common.

The future was pressing hard on the new city, but the past was still visible. Court Hill had the old Court House, the Second Parish (Unitarian) Church and Central Church. On Summer Street were located the American Antiquarian Society, already boasting 15,000 volumes, the new state Lunatic Hospital, and the County Jail, along with several fine homes. The new St. John's Church was on Temple Street. Two miles to the south, on Pakachoag Hill, was the new College of the Holy Cross, a Jesuit institution that would graduate its first class the following year, 1849.

But outside of the central district, Worcester was 90 percent farms, pastures and woods. Dirt roads connected downtown with such distant suburbs as Tatnuck, Pakachoag, Northville (Greendale) and "New Worcester" at what we know as Webster Square.

By 1848, the town had developed a fairly elaborate school system, including nine "infant schools," six "primary schools," three "English" or "grammar" schools and Classical and English High School, which

John Milton Earle (1794-1874), chief owner and editor of the Worcester Spy from 1823-1858, was one of the most influential men in the city for almost 40 years. He served several terms as a state representative, later he was Worcester postmaster and the state commissioner of Indian affairs. (from the collections of the Worcester Historical Museum)

Isaac Davis (1799-1883) held many public offices, including alderman, assessor, chief engineer of the Fire Department, mayor for three terms and state senator. In private life he was a lawyer, banker, president of an insurance company, director of a railroad and longtime member of the First Baptist Church. (from the collections of the Worcester Historical Museum)

Lucy Stone (1818-1893) of Brookfield was one of the country's most eloquent voices for slavery Abolition and women's rights.

Levi Lincoln II (1782-1868) had been governor of Massachusetts, member of the state's Supreme Judicial Court, U.S. Congressman and collector of the Port of Boston. In 1848, after his state and national careers were over, he was elected Worcester's first mayor. (from the collections of the Worcester Historical Museum)

Eli Thayer, founder of the Oread Institute on Castle Street in 1848, was also the driving spirit behind the New England Emigrant Aid Society, which enlisted New Englanders to settle Kansas in the 1850s, in the hope of keeping it a free state.

Edward Winslow Lincoln, son of Levi Lincoln, was Worcester postmaster and then the city's first director of parks and playgrounds, a post he held from 1870 to 1896, when he died. (from the collections of the Worcester Historical Museum)

*Elihu Burritt was Worcester's most celebrated autodidact,
or self-taught person. Known as the "learned blacksmith,"
his knowledge of 50 languages brought him to the
attention of Harvard President Edward Everett, a noted
classical scholar. Burritt's long career as a lecturer took him
throughout the United States and Europe. (from the
collections of the Worcester Historical Museum)*

was cœducational. The "African school" was discontinued a few years before and the system was integrated. The school houses scattered around the town were administered in a decentralized manner, with one school committeeman responsible for each school, including budget, hiring and supervision. Central administration came after the city charter was adopted, but there was no superintendent of schools for several years after that. School authorities estimated that about 3,000 school-age children lived in Worcester, but that only about 2,000 attended school on a regular basis.

Worcester had a cultural life, too, though small by later standards. The Worcester Sacred Music Society began in 1846, the Mozart Society a year or so later. They were forerunners of the Worcester Music Festival, which presented its first concert in 1858 and has been going ever since. Occasional dramatic works had been authorized by the selectmen prior to 1848. Stage plays still had an aura of immorality about them, and only those that carried wholesome messages were condoned. One play ostensibly aimed at the evils of drink caused a considerable discussion. Some thought it made alcohol more enticing, not less.

City status was soon followed by a more relaxed attitude toward stage works and within 20 years or so, Worcester audiences were witnessing a variety of plays, revues and pageants.

Life in the Worcester of 1848 was bustling but primitive, by our terms. Except for the few homes hooked up to the new water system in the center, Worcester residents relied on wells and hand pumps for water. People used privies for human waste disposal, and one of the first ordinances of the new government stipulated that the contents of privies could not be conveyed over the streets, except between the hours of 10 p.m. and "one hour before the rising of the sun" and then only "in a tight box, so that no part of it be dropped on the road...." No open honey wagons, that is.

Another 1848 ordinance sheds a revealing light on old Worcester customs. It decreed that "No person shall throw any carcass of any dead animal into any of the ponds or streams within the City. And no person shall leave any such carcass of any such animal in decay on the surface of the earth, or insufficiently buried therein, near any building nor near any road, highway or street." Other acts prohibited on the public streets included smoking pipes or cigars, playing ball with "bat-sticks," racing horses, coasting on sleds or shooting off firearms. A letter in the *Palladium*, the organ of the Democrats, complained that the new city government was taking all the fun out of life. The writer yearned for the good old days, when people were free to do as they pleased without worrying about fines.

Were we to be transported back to the Worcester of 1848, we probably would be most struck by the gloom of the nights. The streets after sundown were dark as a graveyard, except for the few wick lanterns hung on occasional poles. Homes were, at best, dim places. In 1848, Worcester people lighted their rooms with candles, torches, fireplaces and, possibly, "Betty lamps." Alice Morse Earle described the Betty lamps thus: "They were a shallow receptacle, usually of pewter, iron, or brass... with a projecting nose an inch or two long. When in use, they were filled with tallow or grease, and a wick or twisted rag was placed so that the lighted end could hang on the nose." Kerosene or "coal oil" was still in the future.

But a new and much brighter era of illumination was just around the corner. The Worcester Gas Works was organized shortly after the city charter took effect, and the first street gas lamps were lighted up on June 22, 1849. Sometime after that, gas lines began to be installed in private homes and business offices. But candles and lamps were the main illumination in most homes for another 60 or 70 years.

We would not be impressed by those homes in cold weather. They were drafty and chilly. Although iron heating and cooking stoves were becoming common, some farm houses still relied on fireplaces. Bedrooms were often unheated, as were anterooms.

GRAND ARMY HALL & Formerly BRINLEY HALL 1837-1895.

Brinley Hall (1837-1895) was the city's main auditorium before Mechanics Hall was dedicated in 1857. It was torn down to make room for the new State Mutual Building. (from the collections of the Worcester Historical Museum)

The First Parish, Old South Church, built in 1763, served both as a church and Worcester's Town Hall until 1835. It continued as a church until it was torn down in 1887 to make room for a new city hall.

An early depiction of Mechanics Hall, which was dedicated in 1857. (from the collections of the Worcester Historical Museum)

And we probably would not be enthusiastic about the daily cuisine in most Worcester homes in 1848, nor in the display of foodstuffs in the grocery stores. Staples they had—potatœs, flour, corn meal, salt pork, eggs and the like. But in winter the only fruits available were what had been preserved at harvest time or what had been stored in cellars, such as apples or quinces. The kind of variety that we see every day at the supermarket was beyond imagining. Food in summer was kept cool in ice boxes. Ice wagons were a common sight on Worcester streets.

One thing they did not worry about in those days was cholesterol. Many recipes from the old cookbooks begin with "Take a pound of lard...."

Another thing that would strike us would be how fixed in place most people were then. Worcester residents mostly spent their lives within a mile or two of their homes. A trip to Shrewsbury or Leicester was an event; a journey to Boston out of the question for most, even though the railroad had made it a two-hour trip. Travel was pretty much restricted to those who had enough money for train or stagecoach tickets or livery service. Only a few owned their own horses and carriages.

One mark of the future was the establishment of a telegraph line to Worcester in 1847. Although it was used mostly by the railroads at first, it would become an important source of news transmission. On February 23, 1848, the *Worcester Palladium* announced that "the magnetic telegraph" had carried news of John Quincy Adams' fatal stroke on the floor of the U.S. House of representatives. Worcester newspapers in 1848 included the *Worcester Daily Spy*, and the *Palladium* and the *Aegis*, both weeklies, plus various short-lived sheets such as the *Daily Journal, the True Whig, The Daily Tribune* and publications devoted to special interests, such as temperance. The Whiggish *Spy* was the most liberal, backing Abolition, women's rights and temperance. *The National Aegis*, partly owned and controlled by Mayor Levi Lincoln, was also Whig but pugnaciously at odds with the *Spy* in

1848 on the issue of Abolition and the Free Soil Party. The *Palladium* was the Democrat paper. *The Cataract*, a temperance sheet, was strenuously anti-liquor.

What about medical care? Worcester in 1848 had several doctors, including Dr. John Green, who would one day found the Worcester Free Public Library. Their treatments were mostly blood letting, emetics, purging and blistering, and the prescribing of various herbal medicines. The Worcester County Medical Society, more than a half century old, had its own library. But the city had no hospitals other than the isolation houses where those who had been vaccinated for smallpox were kept, or the "sick rooms" in St. John's Church where the sick and dying Irish immigrants were cared for. However, it did have a medical school—Dr. Calvin Newton's "Botanico-Medical College" on Union Hill. Newton was a quack promoter of the Thomsonian system which held that frequent bowel evacuation was the key to good health. He was expelled from the medical society in 1849 and died two years later, but not before he had fleeced hundreds of students of their money. His "medical college" later became Davis Hall at Worcester Academy.

Medicine as then practiced had other critics. A Joseph Bunstall introduced homeopathy to Worcester just before the town became a city, beginning the long struggle between the homeopaths and "allopaths." Worcester also had various practitioners, including an "Indian and Botanic Physician" who used only roots and herbs, midwives and itinerant purveyors of various quack medicines and untested nostrums. According to Sande Bishop, chronicler of the Worcester medical experience, tonics were advertised to cure "dyspepsia, flatulency, loss of appetite, headach (*sic*), restlessness, ill temper, anxiety, melancholy, costiveness, diarrhea, cholera, fevers, rheumatism, gout, dropsies, the gravel, worms, asthma, consumption, scurvy, ulcers and sores, scorbutic eruptions, common colds, influenza, piles, ague, liver complaints, and diseases of females."

For 50 years, from 1835-1885, the old Town Hall (City Hall after 1848), sat on the Common next to the First Parish Church. This picture was probably taken just before the church was torn down in 1885 to make way for a new City Hall. (from the collections of the Worcester Historical Museum)

The First Parish (Old South) Church was taken down in 1885 to make room for the new City Hall. But for 10 years the site stood vacant while the city government hemmed and hawed. This picture probably was taken about 1890. (from the collections of the Worcester Historical Museum)

View of the Common with the old City Hall at left. After the old First Parish was torn down in 1885, the site was vacant until the new City Hall was built 10 years later.

Although the Worcester of 150 years ago was spared the deadly toll of automobile accidents, it had many menaces to life and limb. Fires and gruesome burns were common, as were accidents involving animals and ordinary farm and factory work. Food poisonings, sometimes fatal, were described in newspaper reports. Drownings, especially in winter, were annual events. Tuberculosis, pneumonia and diptheria were constant concerns. But the greatest fear of all, after smallpox was brought under control, was cholera, curse of the western wagon trains. Although Worcester never had an epidemic, several deaths a year were attributed to cholera.

Another institution taking shape when Levi Lincoln was sworn in as mayor was the Oread, a massive, turreted building on Goat Hill, at the head of what is now Castle Street. Its owner was Eli Thayer, former head of Worcester Academy. At the Oread, Thayer established one of the first women's colleges in Massachusetts with a curriculum modeled after that at Brown University.

The coming Industrial Revolution was not the only phenomenon destined to shake Worcester to its roots. The city also was headed into a whirlwind of social, religious and moral issues that would make Worcester a center of reform movements of national import. Ever since the so-called Second Great Awakening from about 1800 on, religious revivals and passions had periodically lit up the countryside, including Worcester, and those same passions poured into issues like Abolition of slavery, women's rights and, always, the fight against alcoholic drinks and drunkenness. On July 4, 1848, the Sons of Temperance held an impressive Independence Day celebration, with a parade, a brass band, an oration, dozens of prominent guests, and a banquet in the City Hall.

Drunkenness and what to do about it was the first big social issue to shake the land, including Worcester. Alcohol was the heroin and cocaine problem of the last century. The minister of South Church thundered from the pulpit that "During the year 1847, there has been brought to Worcester, over a single railroad, the enormous quantity of fifty-three thousand nine hundred and sixty-seven gallons of intoxicating liquors... and fifty thousand gallons of ale...." He deplored the fact that six Worcester hotels served alcoholic beverages besides "ten other places on our principal streets, where liquors are dealt out to the drunkard." Furthermore, "Among the foreign population of Worcester there were more than sixty places where intoxicating liquors have been bought and sold." Those were the Irish "shebeens" where neighbors dropped in for a convivial hour or two.

Any discussion of drunkenness usually had reference to the Irish, a group that seemed to have more than its share of the problem. In his inaugural address, Mayor Levi Lincoln said that "the influx of immigrants from abroad, which starvation and wretchedness have driven to our shores, has also added greatly to our charge." In 1850, the overseers of the poor reported that the city was caring for 785 indigents at the Poor Farm, 483 of whom were Irish. And in 1848 some leading citizens founded the Worcester Childrens' Friend Society to help alleviate the dreadful poverty and neglect that darkened so many young lives and families. Within a year or two, it had established an orphanage on Pine (now Shrewsbury) Street.

The drive for temperance or prohibition continued throughout the century and beyond. On October 20, 1849, the Reverend Theobald Mathew arrived in Worcester and administered a pledge of abstinence to 400 Irish Catholics. The Father Mathew Mutual Benevolent Total Abstinence Society, established a few weeks later, was a factor in Worcester for the next 40 years.

Another steamy controversy was boiling up around the role of women and women's rights, a relatively new concern hardly even talked about 20 years before. In 1848, at Seneca Falls, N.Y., Elizabeth Cady Stanton and others held a women's rights meeting that tapped a huge pool of female frustration and resentment. Almost overnight, women's rights was on the national agenda, and two years later, in 1850, the

THE WORCESTER COUNTY JAIL

The old Worcester County Jail on Summer Street

*During the Civil War years, the old floating bridge across
Lake Quinsigamond was replaced by a causeway.*

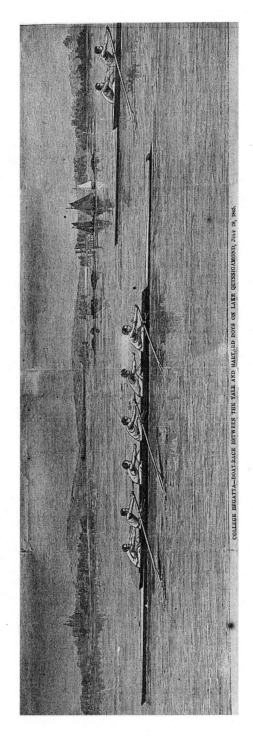

COLLEGE REGATTA—BOAT-RACE BETWEEN THE YALE AND HARVARD BOYS ON LAKE QUINSIGAMOND, JULY 29, 1865.

Yale and Harvard crews battled for first place on Lake Quinsigamond on July 28, 1865.

first National Woman's Rights Convention was held in Worcester. For reasons still unclear, Worcester in the 1840s became the stamping ground for some of the more noted feminists of the time—Abby Kelley Foster, Lucy Stone, Clara Barton, Dorothea Dix and others.

But even the women's rights issue, powerful as it was, was being overtaken by the furious national debate over slavery and Abolition. That issue, which had been breaking out periodically for a generation and more, had been powerfully agitated by the huge territorial additions in the West that had followed the war with Mexico. People who had been silent on slavery in the old South, hoping that it would eventually wither away, suddenly faced the possibility that slavery might spread into the new states, beginning with Kansas. When it looked as if the Whig Party would nominate slaveowner Gen. Zachary Taylor for president in 1848, a Whig-Democrat splinter movement enlisted former President Martin Van Buren to run on a Free Soil ticket.

That split the Whig Party right down the middle, particularly in Worcester. Worcester was a hotbed of argument between the Free Soilers and the "Hunker" or "Cotton" Whigs, so called because they benefited from the cotton trade. The Lincolns were Hunker Whigs. John Milton Earle and many of his friends were Free Soilers. The result was a spectacular blow-up between the two camps, with Mayor Levi Lincoln's *Aegis* making vicious and even libelous attacks on Earle and his newspaper, the *Spy*. "Treason" and "traitor" were among the terms thrown around. At one point, Lincoln publicly demanded that the *Spy* drop his name from its subscription list.

Levi Lincoln II in 1848 was Worcester's most distinguished citizen. Beginning in 1825, he had been elected governor of Massachusetts for eight consecutive one-year terms, a record never since equaled. He had served three terms in the U.S. Congress, had been a justice of the state's Supreme Judicial Court, a state senator, collector for the Port of Boston and president of the Massachusetts Senate. Back in Worcester in retirement, he seemed a shoo-in to become the city's first mayor.

But he ran into unexpected opposition from the temperance lobby and the new class of "mechanics" who were beginning to regard drunkenness in the working class as an obstacle to their entrepreneurial ambitions. The Rev. Rodney Miller, formerly minister of Old South Church and first president of the Temperance Association, got 653 votes to Lincoln's 836. The Lincoln family, which had had its own drinking problems, was not seen as sound on the liquor issue.

Then came the Free Soil controversy. Lincoln and other Whigs battled ferociously against the Whig "traitors" who backed Martin Van Buren, candidate of the Free Soil Party. They brought in Daniel Webster, who orated for three hours on the reasons why Whigs should hang together behind Zachary Taylor. At a big Whig rally at City Hall in September 1848, they listened to another speaker—an Hon. Abraham Lincoln of Illinois, identified by the *Aegis* as the "only Whig member from that State, and a member of the Central Executive Committee at Washington."

Unfortunately, the *Aegis* reporter fell down on the job: "We forbear to give any sketch of the remarks of this gentleman, as we saw among us 'chields' taking notes. For sound conclusive reasoning, and ready wit, it is unsurpassed in the campaign. It was listened to by the crowded audience with an untiring interest, applauded repeatedly during its delivery, and enthusiastically cheered at its close." Historians ever since have muttered darkly about that anonymous scribe who couldn't be bothered with taking down even one quote. The thought of the future Great Emancipator campaigning for a slaveowner against a free soiler is intriguing.

Abraham Lincoln stayed overnight at Levi Lincoln's mansion on Elm Street. They were distantly related. In 1864, Levi Lincoln, as a presidential elector, voted for President Abraham Lincoln.

But in 1848, Levi Lincoln was fading out of political life. He served one term as mayor, was paid salary and expenses of $764.41, and retired with relief from public life at the end of his term.

The Free Soilers lost in 1848, Zachary Taylor was nominated and elected, and Edward Winslow Lincoln, Levi Lincoln's son, was rewarded with the Worcester postmastership. But 1848 ripped the Whig Party in Worcester and elsewhere into rags and tatters. The powerful reform forces that had been boiling up in Worcester County were more and more channelled into the Abolition fight. Abby Kelley Foster and Lucy Stone were as prominent in the campaign against slavery as they were in the women's rights movement. For the next few years, Worcester experienced stormy weather on the political front as the Know-Nothing movement washed over the state and much of the nation, before subsiding in the face of the coming Civil War.

But on April 17, 1848, all seemed rosy as Mayor Levi Lincoln was sworn into office in the old City Hall. According to one account: "It was a very pretty scene. Mayor Lincoln came down from his house at about 10 o'clock, carrying himself with the greatest dignity, as he always did, and at the porch of the City Hall he met with many members of the first city government and received their congratulations."

Lincoln and all those dignitaries could not dream of what lay in store for the new city in the turbulent half-century ahead.

The first Union Station, opened in 1875, finally combined the city's various railroad depots in one place and enabled the city to tear up the Norwich & Worcester railroad tracks across the Common. (from the collections of the Worcester Historical Museum)

WORCESTER IN 1898

When the cornerstone of Worcester's brand new City Hall was laid on September 10, 1897, a group of 86 elderly men sat in places of honor. They had been voters 50 years before, in 1848, when Worcester became a city under a new city charter. Two of them had served on the 1848 Common Council.

Those old men had experienced many changes in that tumultuous half century. They had seen the Know-Nothing movement take over the city government and then collapse in the 1850s. They had witnessed the great fire that destroyed the Merrifeld Mills in 1854. They probably were on hand for the dedication of Mechanics Hall in 1857 and the Worcester Free Public Library a few years later. They noted the founding of the Free Institute of Industrial Science (later WPI) in 1865, and Clark University in 1887. They had no doubt made comments when the first women were elected to Worcester public office in the 1860s. They remembered the old floating bridge over Lake Quinsigamond, replaced by a causeway in the 1860s. The First Parish (Old South) Church on the Common had been torn down in 1887, leaving a vacant space that was filled by the new City Hall 11 years later. Worcester's various train stations and termini had at last been consolidated in a new Union Station at Washington Square, and the Norwich & Worcester tracks and trains no longer ran across the Common. The city's parks and beauty spots, long shabby and neglected, had been transformed by Edward Winslow Lincoln, the first commissioner of public grounds and shade trees. In his 26 years of (unpaid) service to the city, he had rebuilt and beautified the Common, created Elm Park from a piece of scrubby pasture land, planted hundreds of shade trees along city streets, and in general had left parts of Worcester far more pleasant and attractive than they had been.

But the biggest change that those old men had witnessed was the huge number of immigrants to Worcester and the new faces and accents on the streets of the city.

In 1848, Worcester's population had been about 16,000, mostly of English or Irish descent, with the Irish component rapidly increasing. By 1898, after a half century of forced-draft industrialization, the city had six times more people than in 1848. It passed the 100,000 mark in 1895, with thousands more men, women and children arriving every year from every country in Europe, plus Canada. The Canadian French and the English Canadians began to arrive in numbers during the 1860s. The new Europeans came during the 1870s, 1880s, 1890s, and, in fact, would continue right down to the 1920s. A substantial influx from Ireland continued throughout those years.

State census figures for 1895 show that almost 32,000 Worcester residents—nearly one-third of the total—were foreign-born. They included 11,371 born in Ireland, 6,624 born in Sweden and 5,198 born in Canada. Tens of thousands more, of course, were second generation. Half the children enrolled in the public schools were foreign-born or the children of immigrants. The main national groups were Irish, Swedish, French Canadian and English, with smaller contingents of Armenians, Poles, Lithuanians, Syrians, Finns, Norwegians, Assyrians, Germans, Danes, Russians, Ukrainians and Jews from several different places. The big influx of Italians was just beginning, to be followed by a sizable contingent of Greeks and Albanians.

On June 22, 1898, Worcester celebrated its semi-centennial as a city with appropriate hoopla. The *Daily Spy* reported a "Civic and

Trades Procession More than Five Miles in Length" that included more than 6,000 people in the various marching bands, singing groups, lodges, fire departments and religious and social organizations. There was a regatta at Lake Quinsigamond, with many prizes given out by Mayor Rufus B. Dodge. A splendid memorial book, "The Worcester of Eighteen Hundred and Ninety-Eight," 809 pages long, reflected the pride and confidence of the growing city. The introduction asserted that "Few municipalities have within any single half century been more favored in everything which could contribute to material prosperity, local expansion and real advancement in the line of human progress." So it certainly seemed.

Indeed, Worcester was barreling down the bridge to the new century, just two short years away. The schools were grappling with problems like overcrowding, truancy and kids who couldn't speak English very well. Big construction projects were in the works. Some city bigwigs were grumbling about the newly-revised and much-ridiculed system of city government, adopted after noisy controversy. And the people were trying to adjust to a technological revolution that was reshaping their lives at work, at home and at play. It sounds something like what Worcester people faced in 1998.

But if the resemblances between the Worcester of a century ago and today are superficially striking, so are the differences.

Worcester a hundred years ago was a mix of placid countryside and throbbing industry. In the outskirts were dozens of dairy and produce farms. Cows and horses grazed in the fields of Tatnuck, Greendale and along Salisbury Street. But east, north and south of the Common, south along Southbridge and Canterbury streets, north to Lincoln Square and even at distant Barber's Crossing were scores of smoking factories, shops and warehouses where tens of thousands, many just off the boat, toiled daily.

The city's industrial powerhouse had been built on Ichabod Washburn's small wire mill which had blossomed into a huge integrated

STATE MUTUAL ASSURANCE COMPANY BUILDING.

The State Mutual Insurance Company building
was built in 1896.

A view of Main Street at the dawn of the 20th century

On June 22, 1898, Worcester celebrated its first 50 years as a city with spectacular parades down Main Street and water festivities at Lake Quinsigamond. This picture may have been taken from the roof of a building at Harrington Corner, looking north toward Lincoln Square. (from the collections of the Worcester Historical Museum)

wire and steel industry with open hearth blast furnaces. It had spawned a galaxy of firms such as Morgan Construction Company, which made steel rolling mills; Wyman-Gordon Company, which made forgings; and Leland Gifford, machine tool makers. More than 1,000 businesses and industries turned out a vast array of products and services, including thousands of tons of barbed wire to fence in the West. The population, only about 30,000 in 1865, had already passed 100,000 by 1895. The tremendous demand for workers was luring immigrants from more than 25 different European countries.

Thus the settled part of Worcester in 1898 was a crazy quilt of ethnic enclaves. Shrewsbury Street and the "Island" were mostly Irish. Swedes dominated Quinsigamond Village and the north side of Belmont Hill, and were moving out to Greendale, where the Norton Company had located. The French were numerous in the Wall Street-Hamilton Street area. Poles and Ukrainians were moving into the Island district near the gas works. Water Street and Providence Street were heavily Jewish. There was a large settlement of English and Scots near the Whittall Mills on Southbridge Street. The south side of Belmont Street was a mix of Armenians, Finns, Swede-Finns and blacks. There were also small neighborhoods of blacks near John Street and Abbott Street.

But Worcester was not fertile ground for union activity. For some reason, it was never a strong labor town. The efforts of various union organizers usually ran into a solid wall of company opposition, enlightened paternalism and outright blackballing. Worcester had no crippling strikes of the sort that hit Lowell and Pittsburgh and most cities with heavy industry. The lack of a strong labor movement may have worked to the city's advantage, in that many manufacturers in those days preferred to run their plants without strong labor organizations.

The industrial growth and dynamism shown by Worcester a hundred years ago was a challenge to the politicians at City Hall. The city had only recently junked its original charter, adopted in 1848 when Worcester became a city.

In 1893, Mayor Henry Marsh, fed up with the old system, urged the City Council to revise the charter to give the mayor some real executive powers. A charter commission was set up and duly produced a proposal. But by the time the City Council had decreed umpteen revisions, and after the state Legislature had put in its two cents' worth, the charter commission in disgust recommended a "no" vote. The thing passed anyway and served the city reasonably well for almost half a century.

The Worcester of 1898 was full of projects and plans for the future. It was proud of its 11 miles of cobblestoned streets, its 90 miles of asphalt sidewalks and its 2,600 gas and electric street lights. It had 12 public parks covering 367 acres, and 20 public schools, including two high schools. It had a high-pressure water system piped from the Lynde Brook Reservoir in Leicester, serving the factories and many homes downtown. Although there still were many wells and privies in the city, especially in the outlying areas, the water mains were steadily being extended in all directions. Rudimentary sewers were carrying human and industrial waste down the Blackstone River, causing periodic complaints and lawsuits from Millbury and other downstream towns. Huge ice houses on Cœs Pond and other bodies of water stored the tons of winter ice that in summer cooled the milk and cheese in thousands of home ice boxes.

We today would have thought that older Worcester lively, but smoky and unsanitary. Black smoke belched from hundreds of factory smokestacks and thousands of house chimneys. Coal was the fuel of choice, wood being second. Black smoke and cinder particles belched from every locomotive that pulled into Union Station. Most of the streets were rutted and bumpy and trod by thousands of horses every day. Even on those 11 miles of cobblestone, pedestrians had to be careful where they stepped. After all, except for the factories and

The second Union Station to occupy Washington Square was built between 1909 and 1911 and accommodated 162 trains daily in its prime.

The Worcester Art Museum, which opened in 1898, is a splendid building which houses a prestigious art collection. This view is from Salisbury Street.

*Marshall "Major" Taylor,
a Worcester resident from
1895 to 1930, was world
champion bicyclist six times
and the first great black sports
celebrity in the land.*

*This is the locomotive named "Lion" that steamed into
Worcester on July 4, 1835 from Boston, when the Boston
& Worcester Railroad was inaugurated. It was built in
Liverpool and ran between Boston and Worcester for more
than 30 years, compiling a record of 700,000 miles. (from
the collections of the Worcester Historical Museum)*

*Bicyclists on Salisbury Street, with industrial Worcester
in the background. (from the collections of the
Worcester Historical Museum)*

Worcester, Mass. Memorial Hospital.

Memorial Hospital as it looked in 1910.

Worcester Polytechnic Institute, founded in 1865, is the third-oldest private university of engineering and science in the United States.

Founded by the Society of Jesus in 1843, the College of the Holy Cross is the oldest Catholic college in New England.

warehouses on railroad sidings, everything was delivered by horse-drawn conveyance. Coal, ice, lumber, milk, groceries and a thousand other commodities, arrived by horse power. Livery stables did a steady business with folks who needed to get from here to there but owned no horse or carriage. The folks of a century ago accepted their relative immobility, not realizing that the internal combustion engine was about to create the biggest transportation revolution in history.

Actually, the revolution had already begun. The people of Worcester were becoming mobile, no longer restricted to a few blocks from home. The isolated sections of Worcester were being opened up. The Worcester Consolidated Street Railway Company, its last horse trolleys finally put out to pasture, was fast extending the tracks for its new electric streetcars north, south, east and west. For a nickel, people could travel from one corner of the city to the other. For a dime or two, people could travel to Leicester, Spencer, the Brookfields, Clinton, Grafton, Millbury, Webster, Shrewsbury, Westboro and other county towns. They could even go to Boston and Springfield at speeds as high as 40 miles per hour. One casualty of the new system was the old "Dummy Railroad" which ran from Union Station to Lake Park. For the previous 20 years, it had transported thousands of Worcester working people to Lake Quinsigamond on weekends. But the new electric trolleys were quicker, cleaner and more comfortable.

In the 1890s, Quimby & Co., developers, were advertising house lots in the Worcester Highlands, Northlands and Bloomingdale. The Highlands, said the ads, could be reached "by Grafton Street line of cars, Northlands by Chadwick Square and North End electric cars, and Bloomingdale by the line to the Lake."

The new developments, often of three-deckers, were for the rising working class. The more affluent had already built splendid homes along Main Street and Elm Street, on both sides of Belmont Street, on Crown Hill and in the neighborhood of Clark University, which had opened just a few years before. In many of those elegant houses, the rooms were lighted with gas lamps and the maids in the kitchens cooked with gas. But to have gas, you had to be on the gas line. In the 1890s, coal and wood predominated in Worcester homes, and many Worcester folks still did their evening reading and entertaining under the yellow rays of kerosene lamps.

Worcester was also the railroad crossroads of New England. Dozens of trains pulled in and out daily to and from the old Union Station. Steam and soot permeated the shadowed cavern. Even before the automobile, the grade-level intersection of roads and tracks around Washington Square often snarled traffic for blocks. People were saying that the old station was obsolete and should be replaced by a new one, but that didn't happen for another 15 years.

Prime symbol of the new Worcester's hopes and dreams was the new City Hall, dedicated on April 28. With its tower soaring 205 feet above the street, its gleaming granite walls and its magnificent central entrance and staircase, it was a striking contrast to the old brick City Hall on the Front Street side of the Common. That squat building had served Worcester since 1825 as Town Hall and City Hall, but its time had passed. It would be demolished within months.

At ceremonies the previous September, Mayor A.B.R. Sprague had outlined a new era of public service: "As we lay the corner-stone, let us devoutly pray that public extravagance, official corruption, or whatever worketh an abomination or maketh a lie, or even questionable measures shall never find a shelter within these walls. Inspired by all that is true and honest and of good report, may the servants of the people who gather here to conduct the business of this municipality go in and out with the approval of their own consciences and of their fellow citizens, because faithful and intelligent service has been rendered the city, and because the public interest has not been sacrificed to private ends."

Whether the City Hall over the last century has ever been tainted by "questionable measures" is debatable, but there is no mistaking the

*Bancroft Tower was built by Stephen Salisbury III in 1900
in memory of Worcester historian George Bancroft.*

*The popular Shoot-the-Chutes ride at the White City
amusement park (1905-1960) on the shore
of Lake Quinsigamond*

The Locomobile, a steamer, was one of the first automobiles on city streets. The engines were made in Worcester in 1900 and 1901.

The Dead Horse Hill auto race up Stafford Street was an annual event in the early years of the century.

pride that the community took in the splendid new building, which cost the taxpayers $650,000.

Another source of pride was the new Worcester Art Museum on Salisbury Street, dedicated on May 10. That long-awaited dream owed its realization to the generosity of Stephen Salisbury III, who in 1896 had donated the land and $100,000. (After his death in 1905, the Art Museum eventually received millions more). It was destined to become one of the community's crown jewels, noted throughout the world of art.

Other notable buildings were the U.S. Post Office, opened in February 1897, and the Classical and English High School building on Irving Street was only a few years old.

Perhaps more important than all the imposing buildings that adorned Main and Front streets and the campuses of Holy Cross, Clark University and Worcester Polytechnic Institute was a structure whose originator is unknown—the three-decker. Its solid, boxlike shapes were relentlessly lining and defining the new streets all over the east and south sections of the city. Although some sophisticates called it a blight on the landscape, this economical, spacious and honest tenement house helped Worcester to come through the Industrial Revolution with a minimum of social strain. By 1898, three-deckers were housing thousands of Worcester residents, new and established. Thanks to its three-deckers, Worcester was able to avoid the acres of fetid slums that blighted so many booming factory towns of the time. Despite occasional outbreaks of cholera, tuberculosis, diptheria and pneumonia, Worcester seems to have missed the kind of epidemics that devastated some densely-populated cities.

In those days, doctors made house calls. Men with serious illnesses were cared for at City Hospital. Women and children went to the Memorial Hospital founded by Ichabod Washburn and presided over by the formidable Linda Jaquith, superintendent from 1892 to 1929. (It began accepting male patients in 1918). Worcester's Irish, not always feeling welcome at the Yankee-controlled City Hospital or Memorial Hospital, were pleased when, in 1893, the Sisters of Providence established a hospital in an old farmhouse at Vernon and Winthrop streets. The new St. Vincent Hospital treated 104 patients its first year. In 1894 it opened a new, 35-bed hospital next to the old farm house and was on its way to becoming one of the city's main medical establishments.

For those interested in alternative medicine, a new homeopathic hospital based on the principles of Dr. Samuel Hahnemann, a German physician, was just being founded in Worcester. Although the homeopathic concept eventually lost favor (only to be revived 100 years later), Hahnemann remained one of Worcester's leading hospitals right into modern times.

Those suffering from tuberculosis could breathe more easily after reading that the state was about to open a splendid TB asylum in the fresh air heights of Rutland.

Worcester, the "City of Seven Hills" (actually, some have counted at least 15 hills), was also becoming the city of churches. Congregationalists, Episcopalians, Unitarians, Presbyterians, Baptists, Methodists, and Lutherans all boasted impressive houses of worship. Several synagogues, mostly Orthodox, were in use or under construction on the East Side. The city's oldest Catholic Church, St. John's on Temple Street, and St. Paul's, which was to become the cathedral church one day, had been local landmarks for years. But there were a dozen or more newer parishes, many ethnic. Although most began with modest buildings, those led to much grander churches in the next 50 years.

The Worcesterite of 1898 was well informed on current events, local and national. Several lively foreign language newspapers flourished. French-Canadians, for example, read *Le Travailleur* and *L'Opinion Publique*. Swedes had *Svea* and *Skandinavia*, the Finns *Finska Amerikananen*. There were others. In addition there were four main dailies, *The Worcester Telegram, The Evening Gazette, the Worcester Spy*

One of the first photographed views of Worcester

*For a few weeks in 1898, the old and the new City Halls
stood together before the old one was demolished. (from the
collections of the Worcester Historical Museum)*

*The laying of the cornerstone of the new City Hall in
1896. The Chase Building is in the background,
the old City Hall is to the left.*

By 1900, David Hale Fanning's Royal Worcester Corset Company was one of the leading manufacturers of corsets in the country. (from the collections of the Worcester Historical Museum)

The Royal Worcester Corset Company's main stitching room. The company employed more women (more than 1,000) than any other Worcester industry. (from the collections of the Worcester Historical Museum)

Clark University, founded in 1887, is the oldest graduate institution in New England and the second-oldest in the nation. Clark has played a prominent role in the development of psychology and geography as distinguished academic disciplines in the U.S.

The Butman Block on Main Street, between Elm and Pearl streets, was a central business location through much of the 19th century. (from the collections of the Worcester Historical Museum)

and *The Worcester Evening Post*. Two of them were flourishing, two were fading. The *Spy*, Worcester's oldest paper, was falling into genteel decline. The rambunctious *Telegram*, founded only a few years before by Austin P. Cristy, had far surpassed the *Spy* in circulation and was zeroing in for the kill. A fire a few years later finished the older newspaper for good.

Cristy also targeted *The Evening Gazette*, another apparent case of terminal decline. With its circulation down to about 3,000, the *Gazette* was saved at the last minute by a 30-year-old redhead from New Haven named George F. Booth. Booth and a partner bought the ailing daily in 1899 and Booth turned it around with a series of brilliant strokes of journalism. He and Cristy remained bitter rivals for decades. *The Evening Post* was the city's only Democratic newspaper. It survived until 1938, when it was bought by Booth and his partner, Harry G. Stoddard, and folded into the Telegram-Gazette combination.

Newspaper accounts show that, in the 1890s, Worcester was navigating rough political waters. The ethnic, religious and national mix that made up Worcester in 1898—unmatched in any other inland American city of like size—resulted in gritty confrontations and lively political campaigns. Irish Catholics, who had first arrived in Worcester in the 1820s, had become the largest ethnic group by 1895—more than one-third of the population. Resentment against the Irish broke out in the 1890s, when Worcester was torn by an ugly spasm of nativism sparked by the American Protective Association (APA), which feared Catholic infiltration into the public schools. In 1893, despite the best efforts of Stephen Salisbury and the old establishment, the APA launched a campaign to oust School Superintendent Albert Marble for supposedly being too accommodating to Catholic pupils. To the surprise of many, the APA carried the day and Marble was given his walking papers. In the next few years, the political landscape became polarized, with the Irish gradually gaining control of the Worcester Democratic Party. In the election of 1900, Philip O'Connell was (after a tie vote and a rerun election) chosen the first Catholic mayor of Worcester. For years after that, city elections were battlegrounds between the Republican Yankees and Swedes versus the Democratic Irish, with both parties trying to woo the minority groups such as the Italians, French, Poles and Lithuanians.

Worcester's industrial might was vast and growing. Worcester historian Franklin P. Rice wrote in 1898 that "It produces a greater variety of manufactured products than any other city in the United States." That was pretty close to the truth.

Rice noted that "Worcester has the largest wire factory in the world (Washburn & Moen), the largest loom works (Crompton & Knowles) and envelope factories (U.S. Envelope Co.) in the United States." In a few years, Norton Grinding Company would be the largest grinding firm in the country, Graton & Knight would be one of the largest leather belting manufacturers anywhere, the Winslow Skate Company would rank with the biggest, David Hale Fanning's Royal Worcester Corset Company would become a giant, and so would M.J. Whittall's carpet manufacturing empire out near Holy Cross College.

Worcester had been a center of agitation for womens' rights for more than half a century. The first national woman's rights convention was held in Worcester in 1850, and a tradition was founded. By the 1890s, various organizations, including the Worcester Woman's Club, were pushing hard for women's suffrage, and women were being elected regularly to the Worcester School Committee. New employment opportunities were opening up for women as well. The Royal Worcester Corset Company, for example, employed more than 1,000 women as stitchers on its sewing machines. One newspaper story told how a visitor was amazed to see how one girl could handle 12 needles at once.

The sewing machine was one of the new inventions that was creating a technological revolution in the Worcester and the United States of that era. New inventions demanded new skills and procedures. Anyone who has trouble presetting his VCR or installing the newest Windows program on his computer can empathize with the folks who were trying to master the telephone, the typewriter, and the use of electricity all at once 100 years ago, with the automobile just down the road.

Alexander Graham Bell invented the telephone in 1876, and two years later the Worcester Fire Department began installing telephones in its station houses. On May 1, 1879, the Bell Telephone Company, with 75 subscribers, opened Worcester's first telephone exchange in rented offices in the Harrington Block. By 1896, after the telephone company built a new headquarters on Norwich Street, it had about 1,500 subscribers. Ten years later it had more than 9,000. But those early telephones were not trouble-free. They buzzed, crackled and popped, depending on how effectively the wires were grounded. They gave off static electricity shocks. Some were afraid to use them.

Thomas Edison had demonstrated his new incandescent light at Mechanics Hall in 1884, and in 1887 Horace H. Bigelow had staged an electrical extravaganza at the Rink, his famed roller skating arena on Foster Street. By 1897, the Worcester Electric Light Company had built a generating plant on Faraday Street and was supplying more than 750 customers. Electric street lights were gradually replacing the old gas lamps, which had to be individually lighted every night and extinguished every morning.

The rapid growth of electric power and telephones had swathed downtown Worcester in a maze of overhead wires by the 1890s. Some poles had as many as 10 crossbars, each carrying a half dozen lines. It would be years before most of those wires were put underground.

Alhough Ralph Morgan, Charles Crompton, John Speirs and others were driving electric and steam cars around Worcester in the 1890s, the auto was still in its infancy. But the typewriter was becoming accepted and was already revolutionizing office work. An early version of the typewriter, invented in Worcester in 1843 by Charles Thurber, is owned by the Worcester Historical Museum. In 1896 *The Telegram* reported that "The combination of stenography and type writing is a fine specimen of the work of the business women of today… It seems almost as if this department of business life has been created for their especial benefit, since it came just at the time when women were starting out to support themselves, and has opened a field of usefulness which hundreds are hastening to fill." The paper said that 17 type writers (the term then applied to the operators, not the machines) were working at Washburn & Moen, the biggest Worcester company, and that type writers were employed at other firms, at the Court House, and at Worcester City Hall.

Some had problems with the new machines. One young woman told the reporter that she would never learn "all those marks." She has her intellectual descendants in those today who are awed by computers, VCRs, CDs, cellular phones, microwave ovens, home alarm systems, telephone answering machines and all the rest.

Before the Industrial Revolution, women had been limited in their career options. They could be house servants, school teachers or nurses, for the most part. The sewing machine had begun to change that. It was a help in the home, and it provided jobs by the thousands in the garment trades. David Hale Fanning's Royal Corset Company employed 1,000 women stitchers at its huge factory on Grand Street. The typewriter opened up more opportunities. So did the telephone. By 1897, hundreds of women, half a dozen in Worcester, worked the switchboards. In a generation, thousands of women would find jobs with telephone companies.

Worcester had money for entertainment, too. The Worcester Music Festival staged its annual event at Mechanics Hall, which also hosted any number of plays, lectures, musical events, livestock shows and fairs. The city had several theaters, including the Bijou, Worcester Theater and the Front Street Opera House. During most of the theater season, two and sometimes three plays were being performed at once. Famed actors like Sarah Bernhardt, Robert Mantell, John Wilkes Booth and hundreds more trod the boards here.

WORCESTER ACADEMY BUILDINGS.

Worcester Academy (from the collections of the Worcester Historical Museum)

Matthew J. Whittall's Carpet Mills (from the collections of the Worcester Historical Museum)

This view of Mechanics Hall shows the central entrance, which was widened in the early part of the century. The 1970s renovation returned the entrance and facade to its original appearance. (from the collections of the Worcester Historical Museum)

Generations of electric street cars were serviced, stored and painted in the garage of the Worcester Consolidated Street Railway Company near Lincoln Square.

View of the Common and the new City Hall at the dawn of the 20th century.

For the hoi polloi, there were earthier pleasures. The saloon was in its heyday. Worcester had Irish saloons, French saloons, German saloons and "American" saloons. Although the Swedes were supposedly more abstemious than some others, not all were teetotalers. Despite the exhortations of the temperance folks, and despite the occasional years when Worcester voted "dry" on the license question, drinking went on pretty much unabated.

Lake Quinsigamond, served first by the "Dummy Railroad" and later by electric trolleys, was a favorite spot for relaxation, with its canoes, water rides, beaches, lake steamers and regattas. Even before Horace Bigelow built the White City amusement park on the Shrewsbury side in 1905, thousands would descend on the lake on weekends during the summer months to disport themselves. Those in need of refreshment walked across the short bridge to Ramshorn Island, where liquor could be sold and drunk even during Worcester's no-license years. The newspapers occasionally reported raucous behavior at the lake.

There were all kinds of sports, from baseball games at the Oval near Coburn Avenue, to bicycle races at the Velodrome on Shrewsbury Street. Worcester then boasted the world's fastest cyclist, the famous Major Taylor. He was the first great black sports personality in the country, noted on three continents.

Roller skating had been the favorite participant sport throughout the 1880s, with crowds flocking to Bigelow's Rink on Foster Street. But the roller skating craze tapered off in the 1890s, and the Rink gradually fell into disuse. Roller skating was quickly followed by the cycling craze, especially after Taylor arrived in Worcester and began to win races. The new bicycles with their coaster brakes were easy to handle, "even for women." At the YMCA, the National Guard Armory and "the Tech" (WPI) a new sport, basketball, was taking hold.

But the most radical innovation in popular entertainment came on August 28, 1897, when crowds converged on the Worcester Theater on Exchange Street to watch Worcester's first movie—the boxing match between Jim Corbett and Bob Fitzsimmons. According to *The Worcester Telegram*, "The Corbett-Fitzsimmons fight picture was taken by Thomas Edison's new kinetiscope machine at the Ringside in Carson City, Nevada.... It is most interesting to notice the effect of the exhibition upon the audience. It is almost impossible to release the mind from the delusion that a contest is really in progress."

According to one newspaper report, William Brady, the famed impresario, spent $40,000 to bring that first movie to Worcester. He apparently made out all right. Within months, the Bijou Theater on Front Street installed "The Great Biograph Machine" to show movies on a regular basis. Worcester would never be the same, nor would the country.

Worcester residents 100 years ago were reading news stories of events both national and local. One story told how Worcester Chinese were ready to enlist in a New York Chinese regiment for the coming war against Spain. Another praised Mrs. M.S. Allen, who had just established a woman's record for the number of miles traveled by bicycle in the course of a year. Her achievement was 21,026 miles, 4,000 miles better than the old record set two years before. Another new account described the new project of the Svea Gille organization. Svea Gille, the city's largest Scandinavian group, was undertaking to build a replica of the Eiffel Tower for its annual fair in Mechanics Hall. The Eiffel Tower had caught the attention of the world at the Paris Exposition that year. The gold strike in the Klondike was big news.

That is just a glimpse of the Worcester of 100 years ago. We would think its factory neighborhoods smoky and dirty and the working conditions abominable. We would have been appalled by the number of children toiling in those grim, dangerous mills, where the machinery caused frequent bloody accidents. But factory conditions in Worcester were probably better than in England or on the Continent, and they were improving.

Domestic life was improving, too, although it still fell far short of

The Worcester Telegram's new building on Franklin Street, as it appeared in 1914.

In 1886 the Norton Company opened its first plant in Greendale at Barber's Crossing. The former Water Street pottery plant, under new management, was already making grinding wheels. (from the collections of the Worcester Historical Museum)

Court Hill around 1900. The building on the right is the second home of the American Antiquarian Society, now located at Salisbury Street and Park Avenue. (from the collections of the Worcester Historical Museum)

The Court House as rebuilt in 1899. The 1874 addition to the old Court House is at left. (from the collections of the Worcester Historical Museum)

Elm Park, 1921. The great ice storm left thousands of trees stripped and broken.

Elm Park, designed by Olmstead of Central Park and Boston's Emerald Necklace fame, is considered to be the nation's first public park.

*Horace Bigelow's Rink was a
center of many attractions
during the 1880s and 1890s,
including roller skating,
exhibitions, sports shows and
electricity demonstrations.*

*The Oval, near Anna Street and Coburn Avenue, was for
years a main venue for city sports events of various kinds. It
was used as an athletic field by St. John's High School
before the school moved to Shrewsbury. (from the
collections of the Worcester Historical Museum)*

*Putting the Blackstone River underground began in 1849
and was the longest-lasting public works project in
Worcester history. This construction on Green Street
probably dates from 1900 or thereabouts. (from the
collections of the Worcester Historical Museum)*

*View of the yard of the Washburn & Moen Manufacturing
Company in 1882. In 1898, historian Franklin P. Rice
noted that Washburn & Moen was the
largest wire factory in the world.*

even minimal standards of today. The upper and middle classes could rely on live-in help to aid in the daily household tasks. Newspaper advertisements for "Swede girls" or "Nice Irish girls" were common. But in the three-deckers and other worker homes, wives and daughters did the scut work, washing, cooking, cleaning, sewing and all the rest with no help from any power-driven device (although some homes had foot-powered sewing machines). Washing was done by hand in washtubs with washboards. On certain days of the week, clothes lines bloomed with wash all over Worcester. Rugs were periodically taken outdoors and beaten until the dust swirled. But life in Worcester still was better than life in Dublin, Hoganes, Yerevan, Minsk, Abruzzi or most of the hundreds of other places the immigrants had come from.

Worcester in 1898 was a bustling dynamo of a city, a product of the industrial revolution with paternalistic overtones, a collaboration of the working masses with the upper classes in building a community that offered much to all walks of citizens.

Looking back from the vantage point of a century, we can be amazed that so much was accomplished. And in that Worcester, so different from ours in so many ways, we can see the outlines of what was to come.

*Interior and exterior views of Union Station in the
1990s. The grand structure awaits restoration.
(© Brian F. Crowley)*

WORCESTER IN 1998

I f Worcester folks from either 1848 or 1898—or 1948—could visit downtown Worcester today, their first question might be: Where is everybody? There is no bustle on the sidewalks, no throngs leaving shops and factories at noon, no crowds at Harrington Corner, once the crossroads of Worcester, and not much traffic on the downtown streets. Even the Common, nice as it is, would seem to them sparsely used.

They would appreciate the new office buildings, skyscrapers by their standards. But if they ventured to explore the city, they would surely wonder where all the shops, mills, stores and factories had gone. They would wander by once-famous plants boarded up and abandoned, or converted into apartment housing or divided up for various commercial tenants. They would note the lack of noontime factory whistles which once heralded throngs of workers pouring out of the grimy mills. They would be hard put to understand how hundreds and thousands of people were using computers to do their work at home, or watching television for entertainment, leaving so much of downtown Worcester relatively empty.

Worcester in 1998 was a far cry from the industrial powerhouse of 1898, and only a distant echo of the rawboned, rustic new city of 1848, so dedicated to the "mechanic arts." Many of its heavy industries were gone, victims of outside ownership and changing markets. The toll of losses is long—Washburn & Moen, Leland Gifford, Worcester Corset Company, Pullman Standard, Winslow Skates, Worcester

Piano, Curtis & Marble, Reed & Prince, Reed & Prentice, Crompton & Knowles, Worcester Shredded Wheat, Heald Machine, Graton & Knight, Winslow Carpet, and so on. Norton Company, once the pride of local ownership, still employed 2,500 who turned out grinding wheels and related items at its Greendale plant, but under French ownership. Jamesbury, born in Worcester and the product of Worcester ingenuity, was a branch of a Finnish concern. Wyman-Gordon, still an important manufacturer of forgings, had virtually abandoned its Worcester plant for North Grafton. Morgan Construction Company, one of the few old-time firms to buck the trend, still was locally owned, still was headed by a Morgan, and still produced steel rolling mills for a worldwide market.

Some newer manufacturing firms remained—Kennedy Die Castings, Kervick Enterprises, Parker Metal are examples—and manufacturing, for all its stresses and challenges, remained an important part of the Worcester picture. A 1995 study showed that Worcester retained 13,491 jobs in manufacturing, still a substantial number, but 7,000 fewer than in 1985. In 1948, fifty years before, three times as many Worcester workers had been engaged in manufacturing.

In short, Worcester had been transformed—again. The city's major source of jobs in 1998 was the service sector. The largest employer by far was the University of Massachusetts Medical School and Teaching Hospital, with more than 6,000 on its payroll. When its merger with Memorial Health Systems is completed, the combined complex will probably provide 10,000 jobs. The completion of the Medical City complex will most likely bring the number of people working in health care in Worcester to more than 15,000. Such a figure would amaze the Worcester of a century ago, when all the doctors and hospitals together probably did not account for 300 employees, and were only a tiny factor in the total economic picture.

The striking expansion of traditional medical services did not mean the end of nontraditional modes of healing. Acupuncture, chiropractic, hypnotism, ayurvedic treatments, reflexology, Reiki, massage therapy, yoga, aroma therapy and many other procedures were available in Worcester and surrounding towns. Even homeopathy, although no homeopathic medical schools were functioning in the United States, was making a modest comeback in Worcester and the country as a whole.

The Worcester of 1998—most likely foreshadowing the Worcester of the 21st Century—was a complex mixture of manufacturing, retailing, service industries, research and education. Some Worcester workers made steel rolling mills and machine tools and fixed household appliances. Others did new frontier research in biotechnology. Still others serviced and installed computers and office systems and all sorts of modern electronic equipment. Thousands were engaged in the health industry, with its hospitals, clinics, nursing homes and out-patient services. In 1998, Worcester seemed to be adapting to the new times about as well as most old factory cities were. Curiously, given its history as a landlocked place, Worcester in 1988 became a port city, bonded by the U.S. Custom Service as the terminal for thousands of tons of import cargoes from the Far East. The shipments are brought to Worcester by rail via double-stacked rail cars, and distributed throughout New England by truck.

The prior one hundred years had brought many developments and changes. Worcester's population had continued to grow, topping 150,000 in 1912, and reaching its all-time high in 1950, when the U.S. Census showed a count of 203,486. Both World War I and World War II had boosted the city's heavy industries, but a long decline had begun after the end of World War II in 1945. And the suburbanization of America affected the city, too, as scores of families left their three-decker apartments and headed for Shrewsbury, Holden, West Boylston and other nearby towns. The 1970 Census showed a count of 176,572—down 25,000 from its peak and still dropping. At one point,

The Salisbury mansion was located in Lincoln Square from 1772-1932, when it was moved up Highland Street to make room for the new Memorial Auditorium. (from the collections of the Worcester Historical Museum)

Lincoln Square at night, showing the Court House, the Memorial Auditorium and interstate I-290.
(© Brian F. Crowley)

George F. Booth (1870-1955), editor and publisher of the Telegram & Gazette, was a powerful influence in Worcester from 1900-1955.

Sara Robertson, mayor of Worcester, 1982-1983.

*A Worcester Aqueduct Company had been formed in 1845
to pipe water from Bladder Pond to the downtown
neighborhood. (Bladder Pond, an unfortunate designation
for a water supply, was soon renamed Bell Pond.)*

*Swimmers in Bell Pond at the top of Belmont Hill
(© Brian F. Crowley)*

*An aerial view of Lake Quinsigamond. Notice the Route 9
bridge towards the top of the photograph. (from the
collections of the Worcester Historical Museum)*

Worcester's population was probably around 155,000. A slow turnaround began in the 1980s and by 1998, according to U.S. Census projections, Worcester's population was somewhere near 166,000, still the second largest in New England, ahead of Springfield, Providence and Hartford. Some estimated that Worcester would have about 170,000 residents by the year 2000 and perhaps 178,000 by 2020, about what it had in 1920.

Worcester in 1998 was still an ethnic crazy quilt, but with softer edges. The nationalities of 100 years before were pretty much homogenized and were no longer classified as minorities. But there were new groups on Worcester streets—Puerto Ricans, Mexicans, Columbians, Jamaicans, Cubans, Chinese, Vietnamese, Koreans, Cambodians, Laotians, Indians, Pakistanis, etc. A rough estimate of the minority component in 1998 numbered non-Hispanic blacks at 9,000, Hispanics at 22,000, and Asians at 6,500, half of whom were Vietnamese. As had been the case a century before, new immigrants and their families were about 25 percent of the total.

Worcester people from 1948 and 1898 would note many changes in the central downtown business district. The old cluster of department stores, service shops, businesses, and specialty establishments had vanished from Main, Pleasant, Front, Commercial and Franklin Streets. Denholm's, Filene's, MacInnes, Richard Healy, Sherer's, Ware Pratt, Marcus, Barnard & Sumner and other famed merchandising names were gone with the winds of change and the ubiquitous home computer. Most of the city's banks had been swallowed up in megamergers planned in Boston, New York, and various places out of state. Paul Revere Insurance Companies went the same route. Even the city's newspapers, with their long and proud traditions of local ownership and management, had felt the blast. The *Telegram* and *The Evening Gazette* had been bought by the *San Francisco Chronicle* in 1986, and combined into a single morning newspaper. For the first time in more than a century, Worcester was without an afternoon paper. *Worcester Magazine*, a weekly begun in the 1970s, provided an additional source of news and opinion, along with the *Catholic Free Press*, owned by the Catholic diocese. Worcester had become a diocese in 1950, after having been part of the Springfield diocese since 1870. But those who fondly remembered the newspaper tycoons of the past, particularly George F. Booth, sometimes felt that Worcester had lost its central, directing force, leaving a leadership void.

Downtown retailing in 1998 was pretty much confined to a vast mall, The Worcester Common Outlets, elegant and temperature-controlled, but more or less sealed off from downtown life and activity. Great expanses of downtown acreage had been taken for public or quasi-public purposes, including a large Centrum hall, a convention center and a "Medical City" complex, under construction in 1998. The new Public Library, opened in 1964, was deemed too small and inadequate by 1998, and plans were being drawn up for a renovation and large expansion. In 1998, according to the Chamber of Commerce, more than $1 billion in construction projects were underway or being planned.

Except for two expressways, I-290 and I-190, and a new connection from Brosnihan Square to the Massachusetts Turnpike, they city's traffic patterns had not changed much. The causeway across Lake Quinsigamond had been replaced by a bridge in 1917, and that bridge had been modernized in the 1980s to carry two lanes of traffic east and two lanes west.

Worcester's airport, dedicated in 1946, had a new terminal building, dedicated in 1996. But the splendid new terminal was not matched by any notable increase in airport use, and the city in 1998 was puzzling over the dilemma. The airport had been an off-and-on operation ever since it opened in 1946.

Regular daily train service to Boston, long in abeyance, was resumed in 1996 and was an instant success. By 1998, 600 or more Worcesterites were commuting to Boston daily, and a considerable

The Providence & Worcester Railroad and Vernon Hill
(© Brian F. Crowley)

Three-deckers climbing
Vernon Hill

Bancroft Tower, on Bancroft Hill off Beechmont Street, is one of the highest points in the city and resembles a miniature feudal castle. (© Brian F. Crowley)

O'Kane Hall at the College of the Holy Cross (© Brian F. Crowley)

*Looking down Franklin Street—notice the Telegram &
Gazette building on the right. (© Brian F. Crowley)*

Mechanics Hall on Main Street (© Brian F. Crowley)

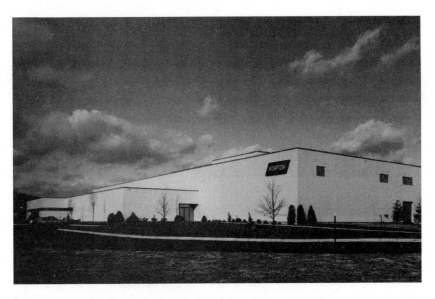

*Norton Company evolved from a 19th-century pottery
shop to a billion-dollar manufacturer of thousands of
industrial products. (from the collections of the
Worcester Historical Museum)*

*An interior view of the
atrium at the Worcester
Common Outlets, where over
100 designer stores offer up to
70% off department store
prices. (© Brian F. Crowley)*

number of people were doing the same thing from the east to Worcester. When planned improvements of tracks and terminals were completed, the Worcester-Boston link seemed destined to get stronger in the years ahead.

Worcester in 1998 was run by a city council-city manager "Plan E" form of government. It had thrown out the old mayor-council-aldermen system in 1947 and had retained the new form with minor changes ever since, although agitation for a "strong mayor" continued. In 1998, the mayor was elected by popular vote and the City Council was comprised of six councilors (including the mayor) elected at large, and five councilors elected from districts. Reformers from 1848 and 1898 would probably be disappointed in the small number of women in elective or other high office. Although Worcester had broken new ground in hosting the first and second national woman's rights conventions in 1850 and 1851, and had elected women to public office as early as 1868, the School Committee and the City Council had long been dominated by men, and still were in 1998. Only one woman—Sara Robertson—had ever been elected mayor.

The municipal election of 1997 may have marked a slight shift away from tradition when an African-American woman was elected to the City Council—the first in the city's history—and another was elected to the School Committee—not the first, but still a rarity.

Visitors from the past would find the physical appearance of the city much changed. Lincoln Square, particularly, had been greatly altered, first in the 1930s when the old Salisbury mansion was moved up to a new location on Highland Street to make way for a splendid new Memorial Auditorium to replace the decrepit Mechanics Hall. Mechanics Hall, once the pride of the city, had fallen on hard times and by the 1930s was mostly being used for boxing and wrestling matches and roller skating. In the 1950s, the Lincoln Square railroad tracks, long a nuisance, were put underground and a traffic rotary installed. In the 1980s, the traffic rotary, often clogged with trucks and cars, was replaced with a modern system of traffic lights and wider intersections. A new fortress-like police station, built in the 1970s, was considered inadequate by 1998.

Ironically by the 1990s, the 1933 Memorial Auditorium was seen as decaying and outdated while Mechanics Hall, built in 1857 and handsomely renovated to the tune of $5 million in the 1970s, became once again the acoustical pride of Worcester, as it had been before the Civil War.

But changes lay ahead. The state's authorization of a $685 million bond for court house construction, with $100 million earmarked for Worcester, foretold the biggest revamping of Lincoln Square since Isaiah Thomas' day. A new Marriott Hotel was being planned for Grove Street, diagonally across from the Armory. The Auditorium, the former Boys Club building, the vocational schools complex, an underground parking garage proposal and the little-used traffic tunnel might all be put into play in a new scheme of things.

Another remarkable renovation taking place in 1998 was that of Union Station, a pre-World War I showpiece fallen into ruin. Plans were to return the old hulk to its pristine elegance, making it once again a transportation and service center that would help revive that end of Shrewsbury Street along with the Harding and Water street neighborhood to the south.

But if downtown Worcester seemed to lack its old vitality and attraction to people, either by day or night, the neighborhoods were taking up some of the slack. Some of them, such as Shrewsbury Street and Highland Street, were lively places during and after hours. Some city planners wondered if the new equation between the city center and the neighborhoods was a temporary situation or something more permanent.

Culturally and intellectually, Worcester was doing well. The Art Museum, a century old, and several times expanded, had become renowned as one of the showplace medium-sized museums in the

Worcester's airport dates back to 1946. Its new terminal building was dedicated in 1996. (© Brian F. Crowley)

The Convention Center at Worcester's Centrum Centre opened in 1997. The entire complex has 100,310 square feet of exhibit space, 23,769 square feet in 11 meeting rooms, and a 14,500-seat arena. These facilities can accommodate almost any type of gathering. (© Brian F. Crowley)

A view of Highland Street/ Route 9 (© Brian F. Crowley)

Worcester's skyline
(© Brian F. Crowley)

A picturesque view of the bridge in Elm Park
(© Brian F. Crowley)

Boynton Hall at WPI
(Worcester Polytechnic
Institute)
(© Brian F. Crowley)

country, with exhibits and programs noted far and wide. The city's eight colleges and universities, including the new University of Massachusetts Medical School and Teaching Hospital, (plus three more colleges in nearby communities) made Worcester second only to Boston in New England in educational fire power. The old Worcester Natural History Society had blossomed into the New England Science Center, a sophisticated enterprise with an omnisphere, a zoo, and a lovely new location on Harrington Way, overlooking Lake Quinsigamond. The American Antiquarian Society, long since removed from Lincoln Square, remained one of the prime centers in the world for North American historical research. And the Higgins Armory continued its displays of 15th century armor and ancient military paraphernalia.

There was a lively cultural scene, with two established professional theaters and several amateur performing groups. The field of music was still distinguished by the Music Festival, heading into its 140th year of classical concerts, once again in Mechanics Hall. Popular music—jazz, bluegrass, rock, grunge, big band, whatever—could be heard at any number of venues, including the fading Auditorium, newly labeled the "Aud." Extravaganzas and major shows were presented in the Centrum, the famously successful all-purpose exhibition hall, hockey rink and entertainment arena built in the 1980s.

Worcester had weathered many changes in the last 100 years. It had undergone a Ku Klux Klan revival complete with riots in the 1920s, an ice storm in 1921 that devastated the parks and city shade trees, a mighty hurricane in 1938 that felled thousands of city trees and damaged scores of buildings, a killer tornado that took 94 lives in 1953, and a major bridge collapse when the Worcester Expressway was being built in the 1950s. But it shook those disasters off and moved ahead. One significant result of the 1953 tornado was the relocation of the demolished Assumption College, founded in 1904, to a scenic new site on Salisbury Street.

In 1998, various public and private organizations were trying to chart the outlook for Worcester after the year 2000. Most planners foresaw a much different Worcester on the horizon. They agreed that the Worcester of 1898 or even the Worcester of 1948 would not return. There would be no flowering of downtown businesses, no return of Harrington Corner as the crossroads of Worcester and Worcester County. Biotechnology and the computer culture seemed destined to become more and more significant here as elsewhere, but few people, either experts or laypeople, professed to know just what the outline and dynamics of the city would be in 2048, 50 years hence.

In 1848, the genius of Ichabod Washburn in inventing the craft of drawing wire had led to Worcester's 19th-century explosion of industrialism and made the city a center of heavy industry.

Is there a new Ichabod Washburn ready to come onstage here? No one knows. The only consensus was that Worcester in 50 years will be a much different city than it had been in 1848, in 1898, or in 1998.

ABOUT THE AUTHOR

Albert B. Southwick, a native of Leicester, MA, was educated in the Leicester public schools, Clark University, and Brown University, where he did advanced studies in history. He served four years in the Navy during World War II, flying land-based and sea-based patrol bombers. After demobilization, he became a civilian historian for the U.S. Seventh Army in Europe.

After returning from Germany in 1952, he worked briefly for the *Providence Journal* before coming to the *Worcester Telegram and Evening Gazette* as an editorial writer. He was chief editorial writer for the newspapers from 1968 to his retirement in 1986.

He has written four books: *The Worcester Club at 100 Years*; *The Johnson Family of Hyde Park & Sag Harbor*; *Once-Told Tales of Worcester County*; and *More Once-Told Tales of Worcester County*. He has written many articles for various newspapers and magazines. In recent years, he has specialized in Worcester, MA history.

He and his wife, Shirley, live in Leicester. They have four children and five grandchildren.